s t u v

An Easy Standard of Pronunciation.

TABLE V.

ANALYSIS OF SOUNDS

IN THE

ENGLISH LANGUAGE, in its mo... ...eas by articulate soun... denotes all sounds by... in such a manner...

H I J
Q R S
Y Z

k l m n
y z &

ffi

H I
P Q R Z
Letters.

15

thought;
t."

unciation.

16   An Easy St...

TABLE I.

LESSON I.

bu	by	ak	ek	ik
cu	cy*	at	et	it
lu	dy	ar	er	ir
u	fy	az	ez	iz
u	ky			

LESSON

	bla	ble	bli
gy	cla	cle	cli
hy	pla	ple	pli
my	lla	lle	fli
ny	va	ve	vi
ry			

LESSON

ty	bra	bre	bri
vy	cra	cre	cri
	pra	pre	pri
	gra	gre	gri
	pha	phe	phi

LESSON

	cha	che	chi	cho
	dra	dre	dri	dro
	fra	fre	fri	fro
	gla	gle	gli	glo

LESSON

| | gla | gle | gli | glo |

An Easy Standard of Pronunciation.   17

LESSON XII.

spla	sple	spli	splo	splu	sply
spra	spre	spri	spro	spru	spry
stra	stre	stri	stro	stru	stry
swa	swe	swi	swo	swu	swy

TABLE II.

...ords of one syllable.

C D E F G H I

For Liana, Joseph, G'Ra, Indigo, Jelani, and Gyasi.
—J.A.

This book is dedicated to one and all who have a thirst for reading
along with the capacity to encourage others.
—B.C.

Photograph of *Lifting the Veil of Ignorance* on page 40 appears courtesy of the George F. Landegger Collection of Alabama Photographs in Carol M. Highsmith's America, Library of Congress, Prints and Photographs Division • Photograph of Booker T. Washington on page 42 copyright © 1903 by Cheynes Studio, Hampton, Va. • Design of *The American Spelling Book* on endpapers used with permission of Applewood Books, Carlisle, Mass. www.awb.com • Text copyright © 2012 by Jabari Asim • Illustrations copyright © 2012 by Bryan Collier • All rights reserved. In accordance with the U.S. Copyright Act of 1976, the scanning, uploading, and electronic sharing of any part of this book without the permission of the publisher is unlawful piracy and theft of the author's intellectual property. If you would like to use material from the book (other than for review purposes), prior written permission must be obtained by contacting the publisher at permissions@hbgusa.com. Thank you for your support of the author's rights. • Little, Brown and Company • Hachette Book Group • 237 Park Avenue, New York, NY 10017 • Visit our website at www.lb-kids.com • Little, Brown and Company is a division of Hachette Book Group, Inc. • The Little, Brown name and logo are trademarks of Hachette Book Group, Inc. • The publisher is not responsible for websites (or their content) that are not owned by the publisher. • First Edition: December 2012 • Library of Congress Cataloging-in-Publication Data • Asim, Jabari, 1962— • Fifty cents and a dream / by Jabari Asim ; illustrated by Bryan Collier. • p. cm. • ISBN 978-0-316-08657-8 • 1. Washington, Booker T., 1856-1915—Childhood and youth—Juvenile literature. 2. African Americans—biography—Juvenile literature. 3. Educators—United States—Biography—Juvenile literature. I. Collier, Bryan, ill. II. Title. • E185.97w4A85 2012 • 370.92—dc23 [B] • 2012007265 • 10 9 8 7 6 5 4 3 2 1 • IM • Printed in China

FIFTY CENTS
and a DREAM
Young Booker T. Washington

By **JABARI ASIM**

Illustrated by **BRYAN COLLIER**

L B

LITTLE, BROWN AND COMPANY

NEW YORK BOSTON

Like any boy,
Booker longed to play, run, and jump
beneath the blue skies and bright sun.

Most of all, he longed to learn.
Booker dreamed
of making friends with words,
setting free the secrets
that lived in books.

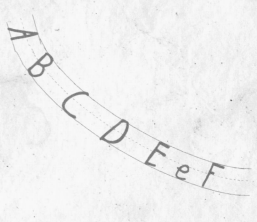

A B C D E e F G H I

The strange marks
marched and danced across the page,
making him smile and laugh with joy.
But slaves like him
were not allowed to read.
A black boy caught with a book
could be whipped—or worse.

When he walked
his master's daughter to school,
he carried her books,
and his fingers would linger
on each of the covers.
He could feel magic
seeping into his hands.

A A A a

B b B b b

Inside, the girl read along
with her classmates.
"A an apple. B a bird."
Booker stayed outdoors
in the Virginia heat
beneath the blue skies and bright sun,
staring through the window.
He listened and dreamed.

1 2 3 4 5 6 7

18

When freedom came,
life was still hard.
Booker's family moved from Virginia
to West Virginia.
He and his brother joined their stepfather
in working at a salt furnace.
Deep in the Kanawha Valley,
he shoveled, hauled, and packed.

Later, at a coal mine in Malden,
miners and machines drilled
thousands of feet into the earth
to reach the coal.
It was hot, dangerous work for grown men
and even more so for boys like Booker.
He had never seen such darkness.

abCdefghijk

Apple

One day, his mother had a surprise:
a spelling book just for him.

Booker went to work on his ABCs,
tracing the strange marks
as they danced across the page.
Soon they began to make sense.
"A an apple. B a bird."
At last, he could read.

AAAa

1 2 3 4 5 6 7

When a young man from Ohio
came to town,
word of the wondrous stranger
spread quickly from cabin to cabin:
a colored man who could read!
Folks loved to gather 'round after work
and listen to him read the daily news.
Young Booker listened, too, and dreamed.

O h i o - - - - - - -

A a B b C c D d E e
F f G g H h I i J j
K K L l M m N n O o
P p Q q R r S s T t U u
V v W w X x Y y Z z

Each morning at dawn,
Booker rose and hurried to work.
He shoveled, hauled, and packed,
then raced to a school for Negroes.
In a tiny, crowded room,
Booker studied his lessons.
"A an apple. B a bird."
Booker listened, learned, and dreamed.
But he wanted more.

more

As a teenager,
he heard talk of a wonderful school
called Hampton Institute.
Negroes could study writing there,
along with farming, science,
and many other things—
and they could read
all the books they wanted.

Booker listened and dreamed.

He had no idea where Hampton was
or how he was going to reach it.
He just knew that he had to get there.

SCHOOL

5¢

10¢

For a year and a half,
Booker worked and saved,
dreaming of school all the while.

He still had very little money
and only a few tattered threads to wear.
His friends and family didn't have much—
a nickel, a quarter, a handkerchief—
but they gave him what they had.

His older neighbors
had spent most of their days in slavery.
They told young Booker
that they never imagined
one of their own
going off to boarding school.

Booker listened,
and carried their dreams with him.

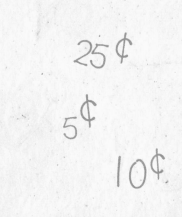

25¢

5¢

10¢

He walked most of the five hundred miles
to Hampton Institute.
It was a journey of many days
through the mountains of Virginia
to reach the sea.
The wind nipped at his weary bones,
and the hard ground
made his feet ache.
But he walked on.

500 miles

82 miles

His money had run out
by the time he reached Richmond,
about eighty-two miles from Hampton.

He was so tired and hungry
that he could barely take another step.
The big city seemed scary and confusing.
So many shadows, and not a friend in sight!

DREAM

forward

Without a single penny in his pocket,
Booker walked the streets
until after midnight.
As he stared at food stands
piled high with fried chicken
and sweet-smelling fruit pies
that made his mouth water,
his empty stomach rumbled
as loud as approaching thunder.
What he wouldn't give for a bite of bread
or a sip of milk!

Trudging beneath the bleak skies
and bitter cold, he could have given up.
Then he imagined the library at Hampton,
magic and mystery lining its shelves.
From deep inside, he heard a voice
urging him to press on.
He listened, and dreamed.

Hampton

5

He found work unloading a ship
and earned enough to buy breakfast.
The men grunted and sang
as they packed, pulled, and hauled.
Their voices reminded Booker
of his days in the salt mine,
of the friends and family
he'd left far behind.

He toted, lifted, and stacked
until his back hurt and his thin clothes
grew damp with sweat.
Days passed.
Little by little, he saved enough
to finish his journey.

When he reached Hampton at last,
the sight of the large brick building
filled his insides with light.
With fifty cents in his pocket
and a dream in his soul,
Booker felt the magic welcome him in.

here

magic

The cost of school
was seventy dollars a year—
far more than fifty cents.
Booker paid his way
by working as a janitor.
Once again, he rose at first light,
sweeping, cleaning, and hauling
before heading to class.

Still, he did not earn enough,
but his hard work inspired others
to help him.
And Booker carried their dreams with him.

Never before had he eaten regular meals
or slept in a bed between two sheets.
Life at Hampton
was all he wanted—and more.

For Booker, his teachers
were the greatest marvels of all.
They were smart and kind,
and they taught their students
to share with others
the wisdom they had gained.
Maybe some students would go on
to build schools of their own.

The way was long

Booker had come a long way
from "A an apple. B a bird."
But even after five hundred miles
and a dream that came true,
Booker's journey was
just beginning.

Sitting at his desk
with a stack of books beside him,
he listened, and dreamed.

About BOOKER T. WASHINGTON

BOOKER T. WASHINGTON (1856–1915) went on to graduate

with honors from Hampton Institute in 1875 before becoming a national leader and one of the best-known African Americans of his time. Today he is remembered as the founder of Tuskegee Institute, which has become a celebrated university. At the time of his death, the campus consisted of over a hundred buildings, more than fifteen hundred students, and an endowment of nearly $2 million.* He learned not only to read books, but also to write them. Of his fourteen books, the best known is his second memoir, *Up from Slavery*.

Lifting the Veil of Ignorance: a statue of Booker T. Washington at Tuskegee University

ADDITIONAL FACTS ABOUT HIS JOURNEY

During Washington's childhood, giving slaves and freed blacks lessons in reading or writing could be punishable by law, per statutes passed by Virginia legislators in 1831 and 1832.

Washington did not describe the exact lessons he overheard in his master's daughter's class, but he likely heard something similar to "*A* an apple, *B* a bird" from *The Little one's ladder*, a primer published when Washington was young. The book his mother later gave him was Noah Webster's *The American Spelling Book*, also known as "the blue back speller." Sample pages from this speller are featured on the endpapers.

At the salt furnace in West Virginia, Washington's stepfather's barrels were marked with *18*, his stepfather's assigned number. This was the first image Washington learned to recognize.

While Washington's journey would be about 385 miles today, according to Google Maps, highways such as U.S. Route 250 and U.S. Route 60 did not exist in 1872. Without these paved roadways, Washington likely would have walked additional miles to navigate through mountainous terrain and other natural obstacles, not to mention any additional miles he might have traveled from getting lost.

Washington's salary as a janitor covered only his room and board, which was ten dollars a month. His entire tuition at Hampton Institute (seventy dollars per year) was paid by Mr. S. Griffitts Morgan of New Bedford, Massachusetts. Brigadier General Samuel C. Armstrong, founder and head of Hampton Institute, helped Washington secure this scholarship.

*Information provided by Tuskegee University

1856—Booker T. Washington is born a slave near Hale's Ford, Virginia, on a tobacco farm owned by James Burroughs.

1861—The Civil War begins.

1865—The Civil War ends, and the states ratify the Thirteenth Amendment, formally abolishing slavery. Washington is emancipated.

1865-1871—Washington begins working in a salt furnace, and later a coal mine, in Malden, West Virginia, in the Kanawha Valley. He attends school for the first time in a local schoolhouse.

1872—Washington starts his five-hundred-mile journey to Hampton Institute.

1875—Washington graduates from Hampton Institute with honors.

1875-1877—Washington teaches at the same school he had attended in Malden, while helping to pay his brothers' tuitions at Hampton Institute.

1879-1881—Washington teaches at Hampton Institute.

1881—Washington converts an old church in Alabama into Tuskegee Institute, which has an initial enrollment of thirty African American students.

1882—Students construct the first building of Tuskegee Institute with bricks they made themselves.

1895—Washington speaks at the Cotton States and International Exposition in Atlanta, Georgia, encouraging cooperation between the white and African American communities. This speech is later called the Atlanta Compromise by Washington's critics.

1896—Washington is the first African American to be presented with an honorary degree from Harvard University.

1900—Washington's first autobiography, *The Story of My Life and Work*, is published. Washington also founds the National Negro Business League.

1901—Washington's second autobiography, *Up from Slavery*, is published and becomes a bestseller. Later in the year, controversy arises after Washington dines with President Theodore Roosevelt at the White House.

1915—Washington dies at home in Tuskegee, Alabama.

AUTHOR'S Note

The photograph from which the puzzle was made

A FEW YEARS AGO, while cleaning out a closet in the home where I grew up, I stumbled upon a long-lost jigsaw puzzle that my parents had given me for Christmas when I was a young boy. The puzzle was a black-and-white portrait of Booker T. Washington. I remember struggling with it during a winter break from school, turning over each piece while snow fell outside my window. Little by little, I assembled it until it once again displayed Washington's stern gaze. The photograph from which the puzzle was made is a commonly circulated image of him, readily accessible on the Internet. Looking at that picture today, I recall how intimidated I felt when I first saw it. Washington appears in the photo as he often did, upright and unsmiling, clad in a stiff collar and crisp lapels, a tie knotted tightly at his throat, an open book resting on his lap. To my young eyes, he looked like a no-nonsense school principal, wise, demanding, and able to look directly into the soul of a mischievous schoolboy.

As I grew older, I learned that Washington was no simple, heroic figure. I discovered that he was a complicated, even controversial, man whose views of Negro advancement often collided with those of W. E. B. Du Bois, his chief rival for black leadership. Over time, Washington came to be seen as a misguided individual who preferred compromise where others wanted direct confrontation, for example, the Atlanta Compromise. By the 1960s, Washington's name had become synonymous with unprincipled accommodation. Writing in the *Washington Post*, critic Jonathan Yardley observed, "Few great Americans have been more cruelly treated by history than Booker Taliaferro Washington. He has been mocked, vilified, and caricatured, yet by any reasonable measure his life was extraordinary."

In recent years, Washington's reputation has been reevaluated. Robert J. Norrell's 2009 biography of Washington, *Up from History*, makes an eloquent case for Washington as a fearless optimist who consistently pursued his goals with his people's best interests in mind. Norrell writes that Washington had risen to become "the most famous and respected black man in America" by the 1890s, mere decades after being born a slave in 1856. As an indication of his national prominence, in 1901 he dined at the White House as a guest of President Theodore Roosevelt, prompting a torrent of hostile press in the South. In addition to founding Tuskegee, lecturing tirelessly around the country, and writing his many books, Washington also established the National Negro Business League, a financial-development organization that still operates today as the National Business League. He died in 1915 at age fifty-nine, having worked himself to exhaustion.

When I began writing this book, I was less concerned with Washington's politics and more interested in his advocacy of hard work, discipline, and self-reliance as effective means of racial uplift. For me, the most fascinating aspect of his quest for self-improvement was his five-hundred-mile journey to Hampton Institute during a time when, as Norrell notes, "travel for an almost penniless young Negro was fraught with stress and uncertainty." Washington's narration of that fateful trip amounted to about four pages in his second autobiography. My task, then, was to expand the few details he provided about his "long, eventful journey" into the epic story of courage and determination that I believed it to be. Relying on *Up from Slavery*, I developed Washington's spare recollections, focusing on the sights, sounds, and sensations he likely experienced during his preparation and his travels. In Washington's words, when he finally arrived at Hampton, he resolved "to let no obstacle prevent me from putting forth the highest effort to fit myself to accomplish the most good in the world." I hope that, in its own small way, this book will inspire similar resolve in those who read it.

—Jabari Asim

ILLUSTRATOR'S Note

THIS STORY ABOUT Booker T. Washington is meant to give us a closer glimpse into his life as a boy born into slavery in the mid-1800s and later freed, and then as a young man left to navigate his way on a long, challenging journey to find higher learning at Hampton Institute. With every footstep Washington took, he had to rely on his great ability to listen and dream.

The images are created in watercolor and collage on paper. One shows young Washington carrying his master's daughter's books to school for her. There, Washington peers through the window of the white-only school, and he longs and dreams for the opportunity to learn and understand those strange markings in the books he carried. Throughout the text, you'll find that Washington continues to listen and dream, which is symbolized by bubbles of light in the art. Also, take note of the map pattern on Washington's shirt, foreshadowing the five-hundred-mile journey that he takes as a young man after hearing about a great school for Negroes where students studied farming, science, drafting, and other great subjects. And that's where he headed with only fifty cents in his pocket. His journey was sometimes cold, scary, and lonely, but with determination, hard work, and help from his friends and family, Booker T. Washington finally arrived and thrived at Hampton Institute.

Booker T. Washington's life serves as a great testimony to the power of literacy, work ethic, and the pursuit of dreams. It represents a steadfast light that shines in many dark places.

—Bryan Collier

BIBLIOGRAPHY

Du Bois, W. E. B., Frederick Douglass, and Booker T. Washington. *Three African-American Classics: Up from Slavery, The Souls of Black Folk, Narrative of the Life of Frederick Douglass*. Mineola, NY: Dover Publications, 2007.

Lewis, David Levering. *W. E. B. Du Bois: Biography of a Race, 1868–1919*. New York: Henry Holt and Company, 1993.

The Little one's ladder, or, First steps in spelling and reading: designed for use in families and schools. New York: G.F. Cooledge, 1858.

Norrell, Robert J. *Up from History: The Life of Booker T. Washington*. Cambridge, MA: The Belknap Press of Harvard University Press, 2009.

Webster, Noah. *The American Spelling Book*. Brattleborough, VT: Holbrook and Fessenden, 1824; reprint, Bedford, MA: Applewood Books.

About this BOOK

This book was edited by Connie Hsu and designed by
Stephanie Bart-Horvath under the art direction of Patti Ann Harris.
The production was supervised by Virginia Lawther,
and the production editor was Christine Ma.

The illustrations for this book were done in watercolor and collage
on 400 lb. Arches watercolor paper. The text was set in Zemke
Hand, and the display type is Sodom Regular and Civil War Type.
The endpapers were reproduced from select pages of
The American Spelling Book, by Noah Webster.